CW01594031

ALL YOU WANT

Grap

(Handwriting Analysis)

VIJAYA KUMAR

New Dawn

NEW DAWN
An imprint of Sterling Publishers (P) Ltd.
A-59 Okhla Industrial Area, Phase-II, New Delhi-110020.
Tel: 6313023, 6320118, 6916165, 6916209
Fax: 91-11-6331241 E-mail: ghai@nde.vsnl.net.in
www.sterlingpublishers.com

All You Wanted to Know About Graphology
©1999, Sterling Publishers Private Limited
ISBN 81 207 2196 9
Reprint 2001

All rights are reserved. No part of this publication may be reproduced, stored in a retrieval system or transmitted, in any form or by any means, mechanical, photocopying, recording or otherwise, without prior written permission of the publisher.

Published by Sterling Publishers Pvt. Ltd., New Delhi-110020.
Lasertypeset by Vikas Compographics, New Delhi-110020.
Printed at Sai Printers, New Delhi-110020.

Contents

Preface

This book is by no means an extensive study by any professional. The data provided in this book are my own interpretations of the subject, gleaned from various books, and presented from a layperson's viewpoint.

The book deals with each aspect of the study, point by point, in a simple language, and serves as a ready reckoner for those who have no time to go through heavy, indepth studies.

The publishers and I hold no responsibility for any discrepancy in the script. We would welcome suggestions or intimation of errors that come to anybody's notice.

Vijaya Kumar

Introduction

Graphology is a scientific study and analysis of handwriting, especially of a person's personality. It may open windows to numerous unexplored areas for anyone interested in practising this skill. It is an exciting and beneficial key to unlocking the potential within you.

Handwriting must be studied, taking into consideration the formation of letters and words, the spacing between letters, words and lines. Since some people write differently at different times, their analysis also differs at these times. And no two handwritings are identical.

As a self-awareness and an improvement tool, graphology is probably the fastest way one can learn about another's personality and behaviour with great accuracy.

Slant Factors

1. A slant denotes the writer's emotional direction and degree of emotional control.
2. Generally, a right-slanted writer leans towards the future, friendships, compliance and extroversion, while a left-slanted one leans back to the past and away from people, toward introversion and self, having more time and energy for creative pursuits.

Moderate Right Slant

1. Communicative.
2. Extrovert.
3. Warm, affectionate and amicable.
4. Sensitive, compassionate and sympathetic.
5. Future orientation.
6. Gregarious.
7. Somewhat impulsive.
8. Expressive.
9. Courageous.
10. Zestful.

for the last few years, they have been lying low. No matter what, they have stuck to their original programme. Let us not forget that we too had once not come to any real

Extreme Right Slant

1. Extremely insecure, and dependent on others.
2. Very impulsive.
3. Unrestrained and bombastic, capable of hysteria.
4. Very passionate.
5. Suspicious.
6. Very expressive.
7. Sensitive.
8. Possessive.
9. Intense.

The Chinese invented printing about a thousand years ago, using characters made of porcelain. In Europe two names are famous in connection with printing: that of

Moderate Left Slant

1. Reflective, withdrawn and independent.
2. Non-sympathetic, non-compassionate, unaffectionate, insensitive and unfriendly.
3. Shy, inhibited, non-communicative.
4. Introvert.
5. Depressed, fearful, anxious.
6. Choosy about materials and things concerning self.

Vast numbers of liny.
plants and animals
float and drift in
the sea. Many of
them are so small
that they can only
be seen under a
microslope. They are
called planktons.

Extreme Left Slant

1. Repressed childhood.
2. Insecure and fearful of life itself.
3. Emotionally withdrawn.
4. Evades reality.
5. Apprehensive of intimacy.
6. Defensive

It measures the angle of the sun's or a star's altitude above the horizon As this angle varies with the distance from the Equator, the information obtained helps the

Vertical Slant

1. Ambivalent
2. Self-controlled.
3. Independent.
4. Self-restrained.
5. Head controls the heart.
6. Matter-of-fact personality.
7. Self-reliant.

When you are asleep, the electrical activity in the brain is quite different from when you are awake. The study of sleep has been made possible by the measurement of brain waves, tiny fluctuations

Irregular Slant

1. Extremely sensitive.
2. Moody and thoughtful.
3. Unpredictable and erratic behaviour.
4. Versatile.
5. Ambivalent.
6. Nervous and excitable.

He does not walk on two feet, but on all four like the animals around him. However, it is also true that the new-born child has a natural and

Size of Script

1. The size of a script projects our self-esteem and self-importance.
2. It depicts the smallness or largeness of our thoughts and life experience.

Small

1. Meticulous and observant.
2. Modest, reserved and restrained.
3. Mentally alert, resourceful thrifty.
4. Lacks self-confidence.

Convenient medicines are those which can be taken or administered easily by the patient himself. Oral medicine and inhalations are convenient and a great deal of research is

Large

1. Bold and aggressive.
2. Ambitious for name, fame and recognition.
3. Enthusiastic.
4. Boastful and extrovert.
5. Lacks concentration and discipline.
6. Strongly motivated, directing others.
7. Confident.
8. Optimistic.

The small, or
even the large,
sweet which some
people suck in
the evening
before going to
sleep, is one
of the greatest

Moderate

1. Conservative, conventional and traditional.
2. Practical and realistic.
3. Moderate in thinking and attitude.
4. Honest.
5. Adaptable.
6. Sincere.

A rainbow appears
in the sky when
there is rain while
the sun is shining.
As the sunlight
passes through the
raindrops at an
angle, the light

Tall

1. Ambitious
2. Far-sighted.
3. Lack of modesty, consideration, tact and objectivity.
4. Observant.

The world's highest
mountain is Mount
Everest, on the
Nepal-Tibet border.
in the eastern side
of the Himalayas. Mount
Everest was named
after Sir George Everest.

Broad

1. Boastful, egoistic and proud.
2. Frank and sociable.
3. Imaginative and artistic.
4. Indiscreet, and lacks discipline and tact.
5. Self-assured.
6. Friendly
7. Spontaneous
8. Broad-minded.

Mercator's new projection thus increased the distances of the lines from each other. While this makes the

Narrow

1. Conservative.
2. Distrustful and suspicious.
3. Economic.
4. Self-controlled and moderate.
5. Shy and passive.
6. Inhibited.
7. An introvert.
8. Selective and critical.

This was originally the padded coat worn beneath a breastplate. Later it became the main garment that a man wore beneath his heavy coat or cloak. From the fifteenth to the seventeenth centuries the

Variable

1. Moody and quick-tempered.
2. Self-centred.
3. Indecisive and inconsistent.
4. Naive and immature.
5. Excitable.
6. Unpredictable.
7. Emotionally off-balance.
8. Inconsistent.
9. Short-tempered.
10. Immature.

The Titanic was the
largest and most
luxurious liner of
her time when she
set out on her
maiden, transatlantic
voyage in April 1912
with 2,200 passengers

Spacing

Letter Spacing — shows the extent to which a writer relies upon cooperation with others.

Close-spaced

1. Repressed.
2. Scared.
3. Selfish.
4. Hostile.
5. Inhibited.
6. Resentful.

The Italian government has now
embarked on the dificult project
of trying to keep this marvel
of medieval and renaissance
architecture and engineering
afloat. To add to this historic
city's problems, much of the
main island is slowly sinking

Wide-spaced

1. Extrovert.
2. Sympathetic.
3. A spendthrift.
4. Considerate.

Clouds vary in shape
according to their
height and tempera-
ture, and they contain
minute drops of
water or ice
particles or a
combination of both.

Word Spacing — shows the degree of contact the writer establishes with his or her immediate environment.

Even Spaces

1. Reasonable.
2. Self-confident.
3. Non-adventurous.
4. Amiable.
5. Well-balanced.

Astronomers have found out a lot about the stars. They know that the stars are very far away, yet shine so brightly. Astronomers

Uneven Spaces

1. Insecure.
2. Spontaneous.
3. Changeable social attitude.
4. Gullible.

Fault-mountains are formed when the earth's crust cracks, or faults, under pressure from inside, and one side of the break is pushed up against the other to form a cliff. They are

Variable

1. Moody.
2. Self-centred.
3. Indecisive.
4. Naive.
5. Excitable.
6. Unpredictable.
7. Emotionally off-balance.
8. Inconsistent.
9. Short-tempered.
10. Immature.

How do stars form? Dust
and gas in the
nebula come together.
Bits of the dust and
gas bump into each
other and get
hot, the way
your hands do
if you rub them hard.

Very Narrow

1. Self-centred.
2. Needs to interact with others.
3. Selfish.
4. Crowds others for attention.
5. Talkative.
6. Insecure.
7. Spontaneous.
8. Introvert.
9. Impulsive.

Rainwater and melted snow collect in hollows in high grounds such as mountains and hills. The water then flows down by the steepest route. The steeper the slope, the faster the river flows. As time passes, the water wears away the ground and the natural path of the river is formed

Very-wide

1. Inhibited, shy and an isolationist.
2. An introvert.
3. Critical.
4. Philosophical.
5. Cultured.
6. Opinionated.
7. Self-cautious.

The dugong is a
gentle, harmless
sea mammal which
basks in the
shallow waters
of the Pacific.
It is about
three metres long

Line Spacing — a reflection of the writer's direction, concern for order, and valuation of time.

Even Line Spacing

1. Well-balanced.
2. Harmonious.
3. Flexible.

Vast numbers of tiny plants and animals float and drift in the sea. Many of them are so small that they can be seen only under a microscope. They are called plankton Animal plankton consists of small creatures such as grubs, sea urchins

Wide Line Spacing

1. Objective.
2. Fearful of contact and closeness.
3. Suspicious.
4. Mentally agile.
5. Not spontaneous.
6. Hostile.
7. Good-mannered.

To skiyak, you
need two narrow,
elongated boats
(like kayaks),
which are worn
like skis. There

Narrow Line Spacing

1. Thrifty and frugal.
2. Fear of isolation and distance.
3. Lack of reserve.
4. Forceful.
5. Creative.

Mendel studied plants, especially the garden pea, and showed that the inherited characteristics were the result of paired elementary units of heridity, which we now call genes. These he symbolised by letters. A characteristic of one parent, such as tallness, which appeared in the progeny to the exclusion of another

Zones

1. The upper zone determines intellect, imagination, spiritualism, intensity, conscience, ambition, creativity and fantasy; the middle zone for daily action, social work, and matters of immediate concern, and the lower for desires and drives.

Upper Zone

Middle Zone

Lower Zone

2. The letters *b, d, h, i, k, l* and *t* in lower case use the middle and upper zones.

she drove like a

big killer. They

looked at her in

astonishment as she

had taken her

hideous and bad

3. The letters *g, j, p, y* and *z* in lower case occupy the middle and lower zones.

giggling and gurgling

jalopy just for joy

privately pay premium

your yearly yield yet

zany and tizzy.

give joy and zip

4. The letter *f* is tri-zonal, and the only lower case letter to use all the three zones.

from far fields further

5. All capital letters use the upper and middle zones, while *g*, *y* and *z* are tri-zonal depending upon each one's style of using capital letters.

Paris Madras Chicago

Grand Yearly Zests

Upper Zone

1. An inflated upper zone reveals one's imagination, spiritualism, intellect and thought.
2. The more flourished or enlarged or twirled, the more extreme is the imagination.
3. A compressed upper zone depicts one's lack of self-image, creativity or imagination, or goals.
4. A narrow, high upper zone indicates cautious thoughts with interest in abstract matters.

1. middleman's land
his hand held

2. middleman's land
his hand held

3. middleman's land
his hand held

4. middleman's land
his hand held.

Middle Zone

1. An inflated middle zone shows immaturity, conceit, a tendency to exaggerate, boredom and a confined feeling of sense.
2. A compressed middle zone shows lack of interest in everyday social and work life.

1. Later studies have shown that the genes are carried

2. Later studies have shown that the genes are carried

Lower Zone

1. An inflated lower zone shows one's need for money, wilfulness, sexual drives that need to be satisfied, and a wastage of time and money.
2. An angular lower loop indicates hostility, uncompromising resentment, and difficulty in sexual gratification.
3. No loops whatsoever suggests materialistic and sexual repression.
4. Very short lower loops indicate that the person is lethargic, and attaches no importance to basic drives or materialism.

1. people's lungs are paralysed
2. go for a fiery and fast days
3. giving off the bright light we need
4. Mary's everyday graduated scale

Pressure

Pressure is the graphologist's measure of the writer's determination, intensity and vitality, and shows the force or lack of it in the person's personality.

Heavy Pressure

1. Aggressive, possessive, short-tempered, abusive, violent, domineering and egoistic.
2. Creative, enthusiastic, sensuous, and enduring.
3. Emotionally strong and deeply committed.
4. A go-getter who is successful.

Agriculture was practised on a larger scale. Simple tools such as hoes and ploughs were made. At first these tools were made of stone

Light Pressure

1. Sensitive, tender, forgiving, adaptable, tolerant and spiritual.
2. Passively indifferent, weak-willed, non-committed and lacks vitality.
3. Physically weak and fragile.
4. Prefers pastel colours.

The best known of these pigs is the white Yorkshire pig, which has a small head and pointed ears. The Berkshire pig was produced in the same way

Medium Pressure

1. Moderately energetic.
2. Cooperative.
3. Sociable.
4. Calm and collected.
5. Shuns extremes and is balanced mentally.

When snow comes
into contact with
salt it does not
freeze. If snow is
expected, or just
fallen, lorries go
out to spread a
mixture of grit
and salt on the

General Types

1. There are four kinds of connecting strokes — garland, arcade, angular and threaded.
2. The garland, a rounded and cuplike stroke, suggests receptivity, and openness to all influences.
3. The arcade, an arched stroke, shows the person to be artistic and one seeking protection.
4. The angular stroke suggests irresolution or discomfort.

5. The threaded stroke reveals a person who dislikes being categorised, and has an intuitive capacity for attaining temporary identification.

GARLAND

A deep garland shows one to be depressive, indifferent, gullible, insecure, passive, contemplative, sympathetic, conventional , lacking restraint and wanting acceptance by others.

A shallow garland suggests one to be reckless, unrestrained, superficial, amiable and well-mannered.

A moderate one shows one to be charming, gracious, flexible, kind, extrovert, diplomatic, careless, and lazy.

Machines provide more power to do work with, and enable it to be done faster. In former times

ARCADE

A moderate arcade shows one to be creative, artistic, meditative, gentle, protective, poised, shy, formal, proud and authoritative.

A flat one means he is scheming, secretive, pretentious, gullible, eccentric and defensive.

created for man's
welfare. Others
were used as
weapons of war.
Guns, swords,
cannon, tanks,
submarines, bomb

ANGULAR

A moderate angle shows one to analytical, shrewd, logical, competitive, firm, steadfast, determined to be a success, ambitious, energetic, determined, excitable, disciplined, persistent and idealistic.

A flat one suggests that he is aggressive, cold-blooded, intolerant, dissatisfied, stubborn, self-centred, critical, forceful, slow and thorough.

must still eat
a good deal of
meat, or other
form of protein,
and vegetables.
If they cut these

THREADED

A well-threaded stroks shows versatility, perception, intuition, intelligence, independence, seeking appreciation rather than reward.

A badly-threaded stroke means he is indecisive, unpredictable, in-secure, nervous, impatient, fearful, cunning, perceptive, insightful and crafty.

Control of body

temperature is exercised

by a centre in the

brain which ensures

that a balance exists

between heat loss and

Individual Letters

1. The conventional forms of the letters indicate a conventional and orthodox behaviour.
2. The flourished, ornamental or decorative form depicts a creative and artistic flair.
3. Weird and unusual forms reveal an eccentric and weird behaviour.

CAPITALS

1. Capital letters denote the image that the writer likes to project.
2. The greater the size of the capitals, the greater the pride, the confidence , and the vanity of the writer.
3. Ornamental capitals represent ostentation and self-consciousness.
4. Printed capitals show that one is constructive.

Capital Letter 'I'

Inflated : Egoistic, proud, vain, creative, imaginative and impressive.

Deflated : Timid and repressed.

Left-tilting : Introvert, mistrustful, cautious, suspicious, insecure, and defensive.

Right-tilting : Extrovert, dependent on others, needs attention, praise, affection and approval.

Vertical : Independent, unemotional, loves privacy.

Printed 'I' : Straightforward, simple, intelligent, modest and versatile.

Inflated

Deflated

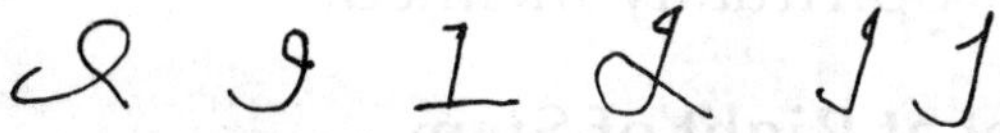

Left-tilting

Right-tilting

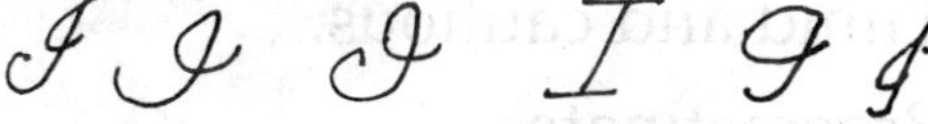

Vertical

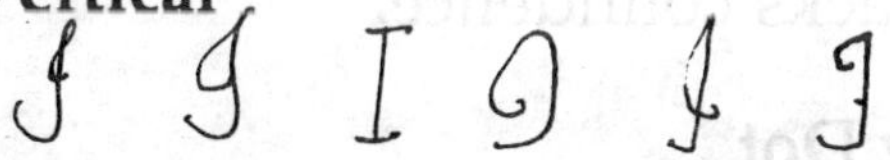

Printed 'I'

Small Letter 'i'

Dot High above Stem

1. Imaginative and a dreamer.
2. Spiritually inclined.

Dot at Right of Stem

1. Fast thinker.
2. Impulsive and Impatient.

Dot at Left of Stem

1. Timid and cautious.
2. Procrastinates.
3. Lacks confidence.

Wavy Dot

1. Good sense of humour.
2. Fun-loving.

Dot High above Stem

spiritual, timid,

Dot at Right of Stem

did the right thing

Dot at Left of Stem

did the right thing

Wavy Dot

did the right thing

Circled Dot

1. Loyal.
2. Faddish, and needs attention.
3. Imaginative and artistic.

Absence of Dot

1. Absent-minded, with poor memory.
2. Careless.

Flying 'v' Dot

1. Sarcastic, cruel, irritable.
2. Domineering.

Tented Dot

1. Critical, brutal.
2. Short-tempered.

Circled Dot

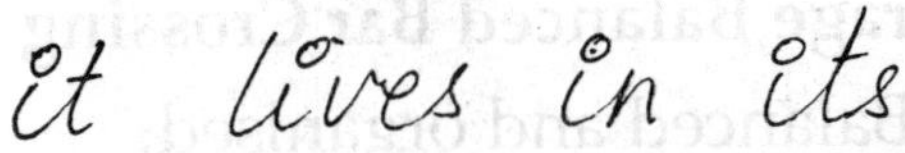

Absence of Dot

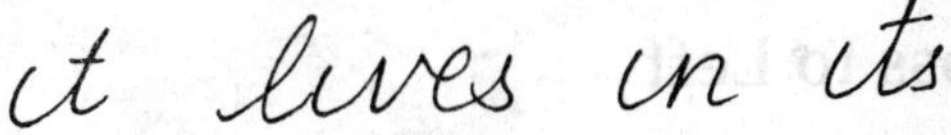

Flying 'v' Dot

Tented Dot

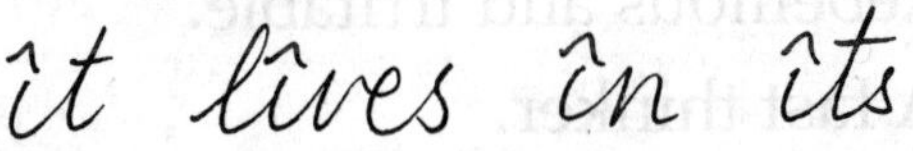

Letter 't'

Average Balanced Bar Crossing

1. Balanced and organised.
2. Self-controlled, calm and firm.
3. Precise.

Cross to Left

1. Procrastinates.
2. Indecisive.
3. Lives in the past.

Cross to Right

1. Impulsive and tactless.
2. Enthusiastic and energetic.
3. Rebellious and irritable.
4. A fast thinker.

Average Balanced Bar Crossing

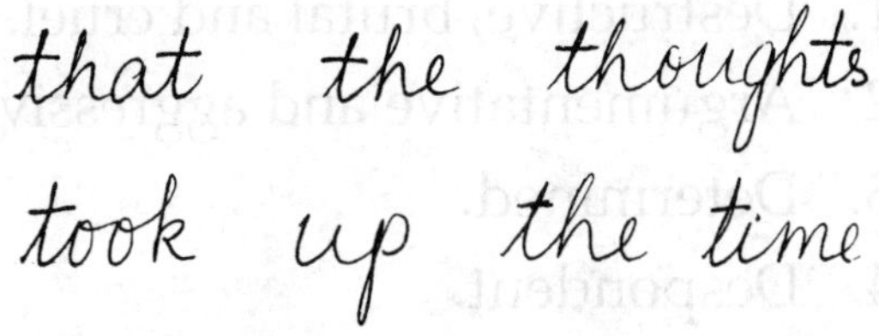

Cross to Left

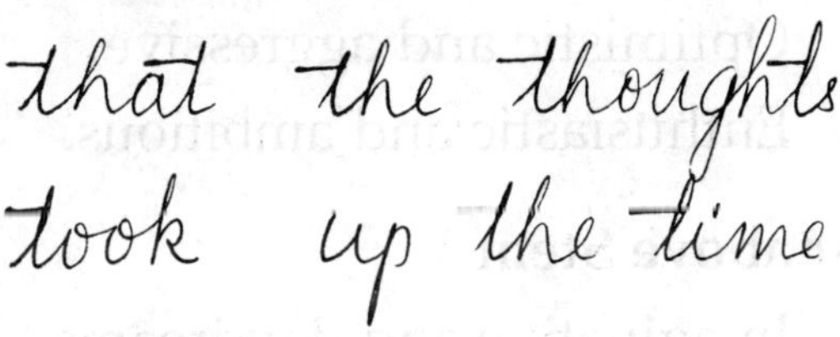

Cross to Right

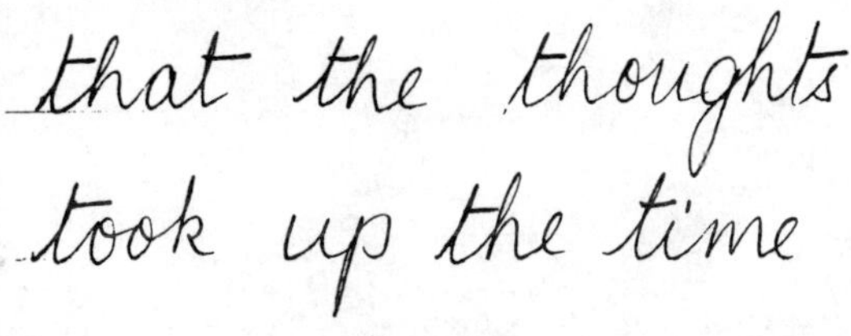

Down-slanted

1. Destructive, brutal and cruel.
2. Argumentative and aggressive.
3. Determined.
4. Despondent.

Up-slanted

1. Optimistic and aggressive.
2. Enthusiastic and ambitious.

Bar above Stem

1. Imaginative and daydreams.
2. Unrealistic goals, and spiritual.

Down-slanted

the truth of the

matter is that

Up-slanted

the truth of the

matter is that

Bar above Stem

The truth of The

matter is That

Low Bar on the Stem

1. Inferiority complex.
2. Low goals.
3. Patient and humble.
4. Self-doubter.

Short Bar

1. Underachiever.
2. Lacks drive and will-power.

Long Bar

1. Enthusiastic and ambitious.
2. Bold and energetic.
3. Confident and bossy.

Low Bar on the Stem

the terrible thoughts

that tell you the

Short Bar

the terrible thoughts

that tell you that

Long Bar

the terrible thoughts

that tell you that

Absent Bar

1. Absent-minded.
2. Careless and unattentive to details.
3. Hasty and rebellious.

Wavy Bar

1. Humorous and good-natured.
2. Intuitive.
3. Frivolous and wishy-washy.

Starlike t

1. Sense of responsibility.
2. Stubborn and sensitive.

Tented

1. Defensive and cautious.

Absent Bar

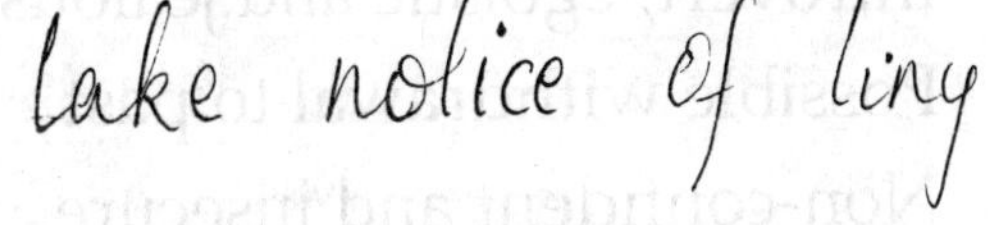

Wavy Bar

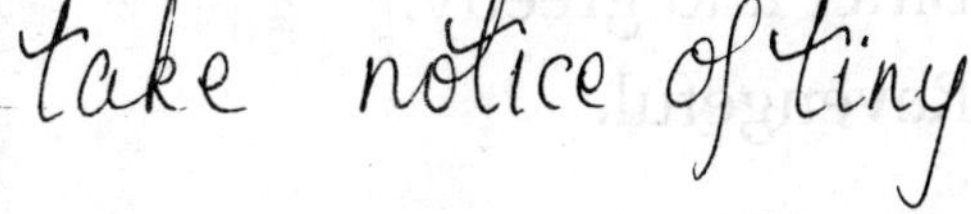

Starlike t

Tented

Crossing Back

1. Introvert, egoistic and jealous.
2. Possible withdrawal to past.
3. Non-confident and insecure.

Down-turned Hook

1. Bitter and greedy.
2. Revengeful.

Upturned Hook

1. Stubborn.
2. Tenacious.

Looped Stem

1. Sensitive.
2. Articulate.
3. Bothered by criticism.

Crossing Back

together at the turn

Down-turned Hook

together at the turn

Upturned Hook

together at the turn

Looped Stem

together at the turn

LETTER 'a' AND 'o'

Double-looped

1. Dishonest to self and others.
2. Insincere, shy and crafty.

Open at Top

1. Talkative, open-minded, can't keep a secret.
2. Honest, sincere and generous.
3. Reticent and cautious.

Open at Bottom

1. Dishonest and an embezzler.

Closed and clean

1. Honest, reserved and secretive.

Double-looped

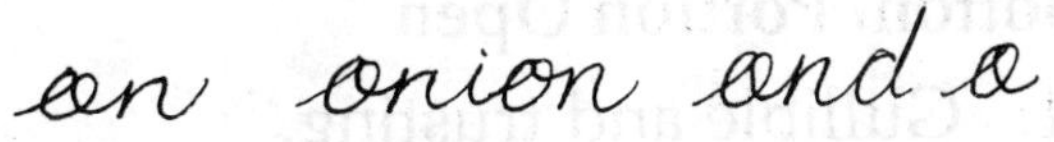

Open at Top

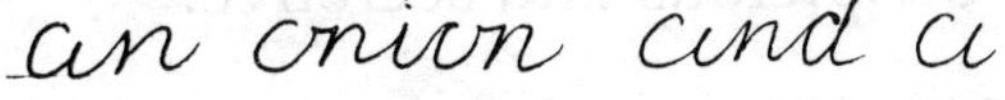

Open at Bottom

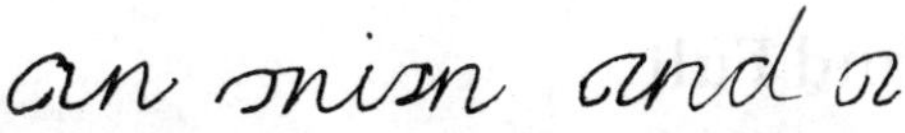

Closed and clean

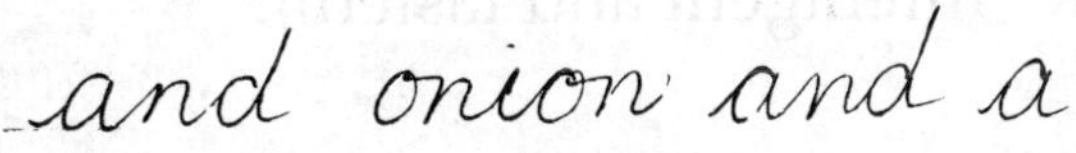

Letter 'b'

Bottom Portion Open

1. Gullible and trusting.

Bottom Portion Closed

1. Cautious, business minded.
2. Suspicious and secretive.

Tall and Narrow

1. Idealistic or religious.
2. Unexpressive.

Short and Full

1. Humble and self-loving.

Without Upper Loop

1. Intelligent and tasteful.

Bottom Portion Open

but buttresses better

Bottom Portion Closed

but buttresses better

Tall and Narrow

but buttresses better

Short and Full

but buttresses better

Without Upper Loop

but buttresses better

Letter 'c'

Crowns or Loops

1. Vain and pretentious.
2. Rigid.
3. May be artistic.

Beginning Stroke

1. Ambitious for success.

Plain

1. Idealistic.
2. Simple and gracious.

Crowns or Loops

creative creatures

call crafted cases

Beginning Stroke

creative creatures

call crafted cases

Plain

creative creatures

call crafted cases

LETTER 'd'

Loopy Stem

1. Sensitive and imaginative.

Tall, Unlooped Stem

1. Idealistic and independent.
2. Dignified and proud.

Short, Unlooped Stem

1. Modest and humble
2. Cautious and reduced concentration.

Tall and Wide Loop

1. Very sensitive.
2. Vain, arrogant and conceited.

Loopy Stem

drop dead and

Tall, Unlooped Stem

drop dead and

Short, Unlooped Stem

drop dead and

Tall and Wide Loop

drop dead and

Bottom Open

1. Unreliable.
2. Dishonest.

Body Closed

1. Secretive about affairs.

Left Flag

1. Protective, musical, creative.

Bottom Open

dark deeds that
defy dealing and

Body Closed

dark deeds that
defy dealing and

Left Flag

dark deeds that
defy dealing and

Letter 'e'

Closed Loop

1. Critical and sceptical.
2. Quick thinker.
3. Suspicious and secretive.

Broad Loop

1. Broad-minded.
2. Blunt and outspoken.
3. Talkative.

Greek 'e'

1. Cultured
2. Refined and aesthetic.

Narrow Loop

1. Critical.
2. Narrow-minded.

Closed Loop

earmarked ends

Broad Loop

earmarked ends

Greek 'e'

earmarked ends

Narrow Loop

earmarked ends

Letter 'f'

Balanced Upper and Lower Parts

1. Well-organised and planned.
2. Balanced and poised.

Absent Upper Loop

1. Self-opinionated.
2. Practical.

Large Lower Loop

1. Active and energetic.

Large Upper Loop

1. Articulate.

Balanced Upper and Lower Parts

Absent Upper Loop

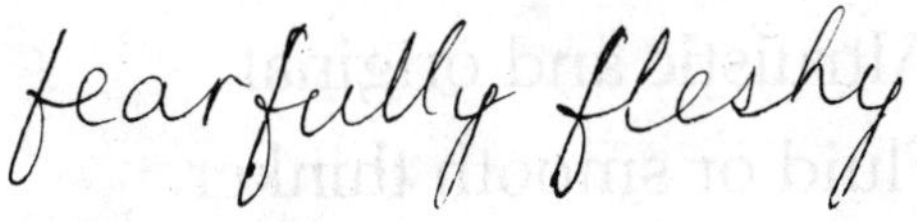

Large Lower Loop

Large Upper Loop

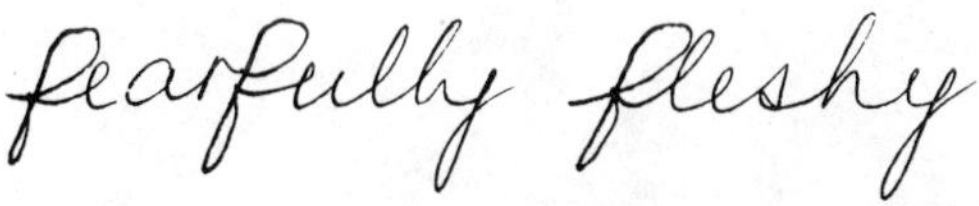

Angular

1. Resentful and stubborn.
2. Opinionated.
3. Uncompromising.

Fluid Form

1. Altruistic and original.
2. Fluid or smooth thinker.
3. Pleasure-loving.

Cross Form

1. High concentration.
2. Fatalism.

Angular

for fear of falling
off the first free

Fluid Form

for fear of falling
off the first free

Cross Form

for fear of falling
off the first free

LETTERS 'g', 'q', 'y' AND 'z'

Long Stem

1. Narrow-minded.

Rounded Full Loop

1. Gregarious and loyal.
2. Interested in saving money.

Absent Loop

1. Practical and aggressive.

Triangular Stem

1. Opinionated and critical.
2. Tenacious, compulsive, aggressive.

Resembling Number '8'

1. Intellectual, altruistic, adaptable.
2. Understanding.

Long Stem

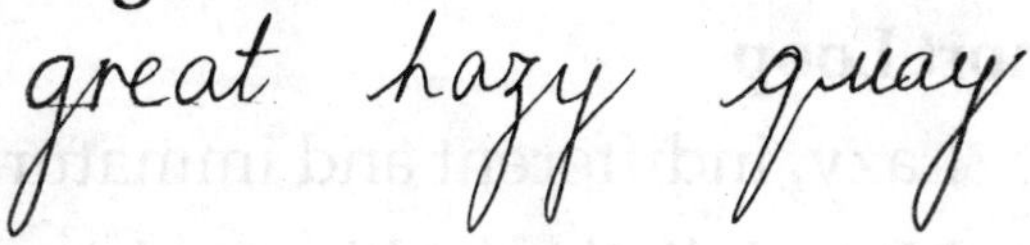

Rounded Full Loop

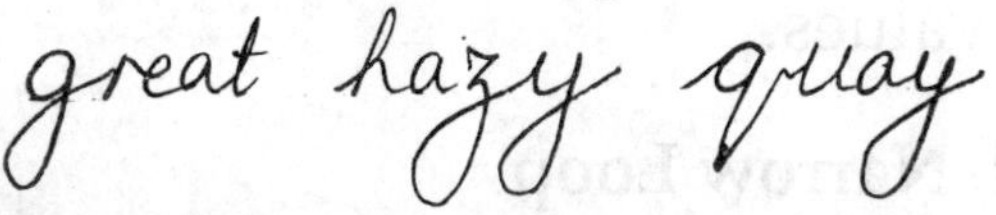

Absent Loop

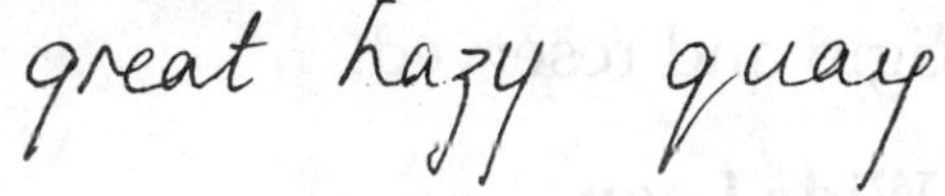

Triangular Stem

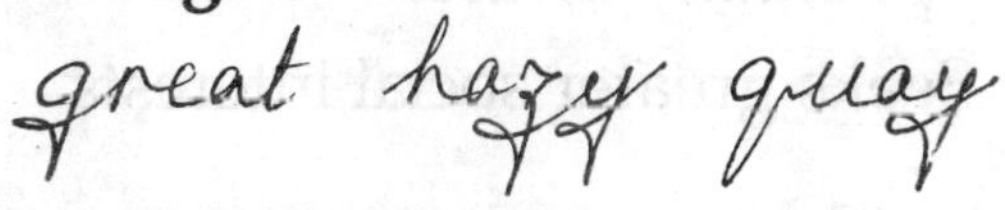

Resembling Number '8'

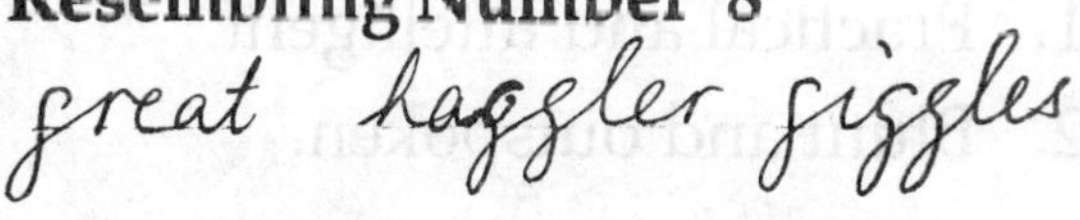

Letter 'h', 'k' and 'l'

Short Loop

1. Lazy, indifferent and immature.
2. Materialistic, lacking spiritual values.

Tall, Narrow Loop

1. Spiritual and high mental reach.
2. Rigid and reserved.

Tall, Wide Loop

1. Spiritually aware.
2. Seeks greater social interests.

Absent Loop

1. Practical and intelligent.
2. Blunt and outspoken.

Short Loop

hooked handles

Tall, Narrow Loop

hooked handles

Tall, Wide Loop

hooked handles

Absent Loop

hooked handles

Letters 'm' and 'n'

Rounded

1. Slow, lazy and immature.
2. Cautious, gentle, analytical.

Peaked

1. A bright thinker with a sharp mind.

Initial Stroke Large and Flourishing

1. Diplomatic, executive ability.

Final Stroke Higher than Others

1. Eccentric and stubborn.

Graceful First Stroke

1. Good-natured and amiable

Rounded

more often than

Peaked

more often than

Initial Stroke Large and Flourishing

more often than

Final Stroke Higher than Others

more often than

Graceful First Stroke

more often than

LETTER 'p'

Large Loop

1. Physically active.
2. Likes sports and dances.

Short Upper Stem

1. Expects rewards.
2. Unwilling to go out of the way.

High Upper Stem

1. Charitable.
2. Toils without expectations.

Open Body

1. Talkative, relaxed, a spendthrift.

Large Loop

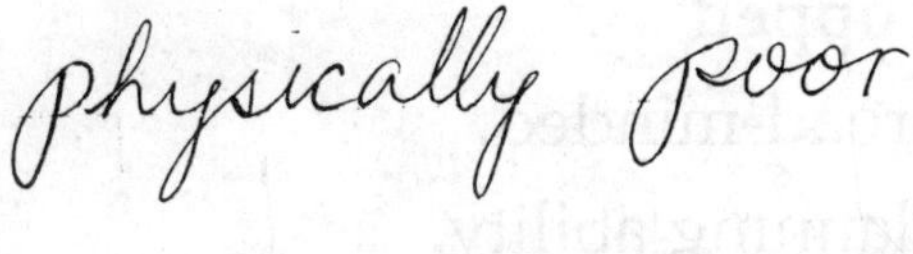

Short Upper Stem

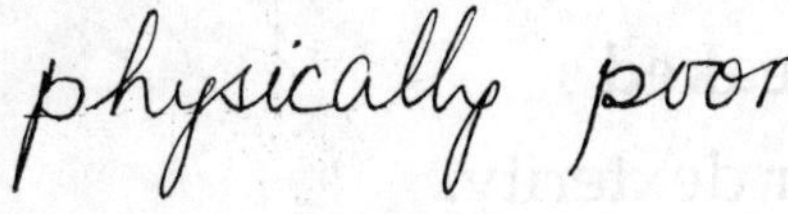

High Upper Stem

Open Body

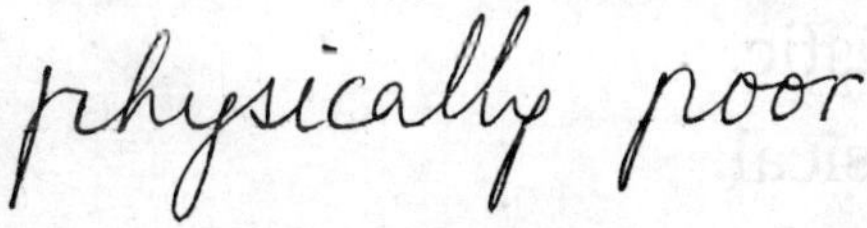

LETTER 'r'

Flat Topped

1. Broad-minded.
2. Planning ability.
3. Skilful with tools.

Double Peaked

1. Finger dexterity.
2. Perceptive and clever.

Initial Stroke Looped

1. Proud and stubborn.
2. Sings to self.

Parochial 'r'

1. Artistic.
2. Musical.
3. Suppressed thinking

Flat Topped

Double Peaked

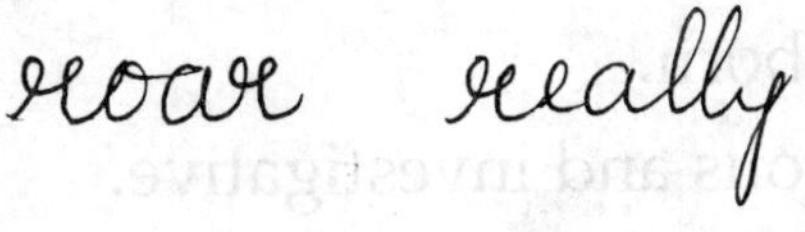

Initial Stroke Looped

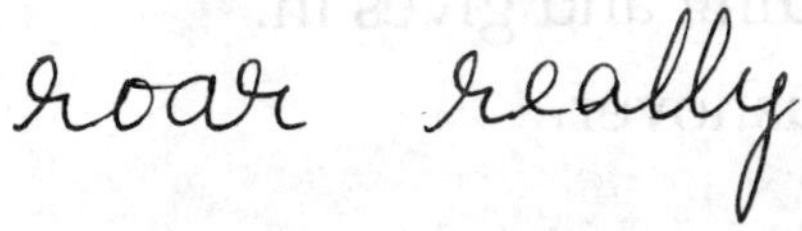

Parochial 'r'

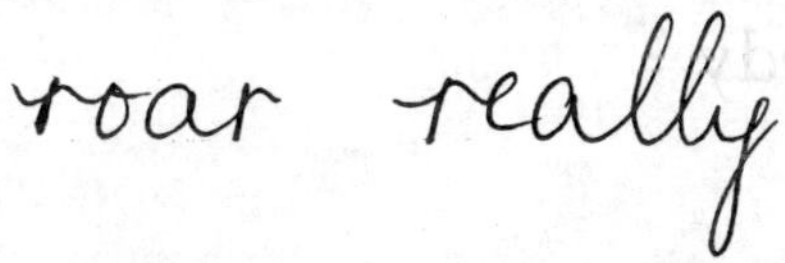

Letter 's'

Printed 's'

1. Artistic.
2. Cultured.

Upper Peak

1. Stubborn.
2. Curious and investigative.

Rounded Top

1. Yielding and gives in.
2. A pushover.

Enrolled

1. Shrewd.
2. Greedy.

Printed 's'

some say she

Upper Peak

some say she

Rounded Top

some say she

Enrolled

some say she

LOOPS

1. The height and width of a loop depicts one's mental interests and spiritualism, and one's social and gregarious nature, respectively.
2. Loops in moderation indicate mental stability and well-being.
3. Exaggerated loops suggest that the person is an extrovert, sympathetic, social, intuitive, impulsive and compassionate.
4. Scanty and narrow loops denote repressed emotional feelings.

he feels his
face crinkling,
making him
look crinkled
and wrinkled,
because his body

KNOTS, HOOKS AND CLAWS

1. Knotted letters depict a person who is tenacious, persistent and logical.
2. The upward turning claws and hooks show a person to be materialistic, greedy, vindictive, and cannot stand opposition.
3. The downward turning claws and hooks show a person to be forceful and bitter, apart from having all the traits that the upturned claws and hooks show.

you can always
say that goings
by what people
think of these
various ways

Signatures

1. A signature is the image that one likes to project to the outer world.
2. A signature is not necessarily the way one is, especially when its style differs from the main body of the writing.

Smaller than Script

1. Introvert and shy.
2. Unpretentious, humble and submissive.
3. Oversensitive and insecure.
4. Calm and mild.

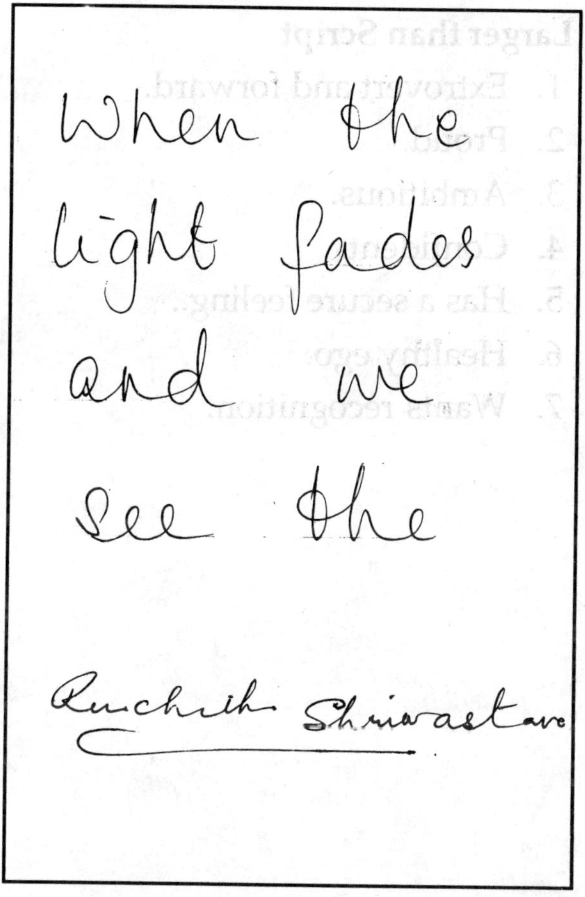
When the
light fades
and we
see the

Larger than Script

1. Extrovert and forward.
2. Proud.
3. Ambitious.
4. Confident.
5. Has a secure feeling..
6. Healthy ego.
7. Wants recognition.

else we'll never know what hit us like a ton of bricks!

Corina Corpus

Left Slanting with Script Right-slanting

1. Pretentious.
2. Projects an image which is not true.

Many are the
ways of finding
the much needed
information and

Right-slanting with Script Left-slanting or Vertical

1. Pretends to be an extrovert.
2. A private person.

Corns and callouses are lumps or patches of hard skin, often painful, which can

Vertical with Script Vertical or Left-slanting

1. Appears controlled to the world.
2. Balanced.
3. Down to earth.
4. Self-confident.

retina is the delicate tissue containing the photo receptors. The effect is much similar

Sandhya Rani

Illegible with Legible Writing

1. A good communicator but likes to be incognito.
2. Could be secretive, insecure and impatient.
3. Hostile.
4. Egoistic.
5. Eccentric.
6. Inconsiderate.

With both eyes
in front, their
separate fields
of vision overlap

Illegible with Illegible Writing

1. Unconcerned.
2. Dishonest.
3. Egocentric.
4. Impatient.

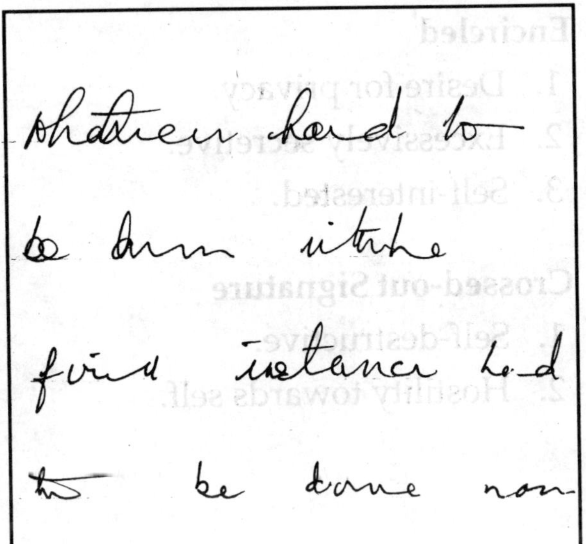

Encircled

1. Desire for privacy.
2. Excessively secretive.
3. Self-interested.

Crossed-out Signature

1. Self-destructive.
2. Hostility towards self.

1.

2.

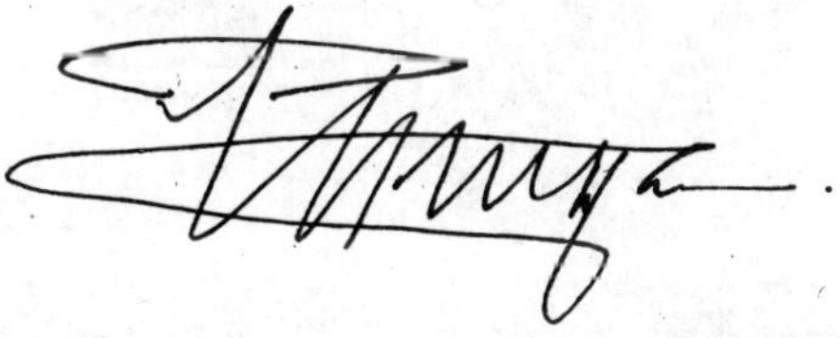

Margins

1. Margins show the writer's degree of economy, consistency, tolerance, desire for esteem, and urge for acceptance.
2. Well-spaced margins denote an intelligent arrangement of time and space accompanied by favourable organisation.

Wide Upper Margin

1. Modest and formal.
2. Reserved and withdrawn.

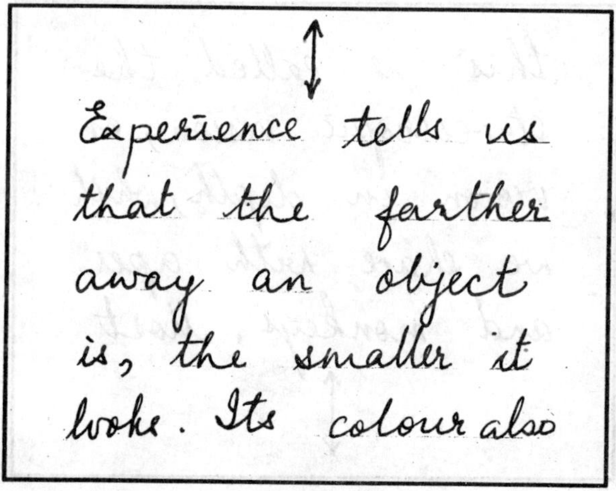

Wide Lower Margin

1. Idealistic.
2. Superficial.
3. Aloof and reserved.
4. Sexual or emotional trauma.

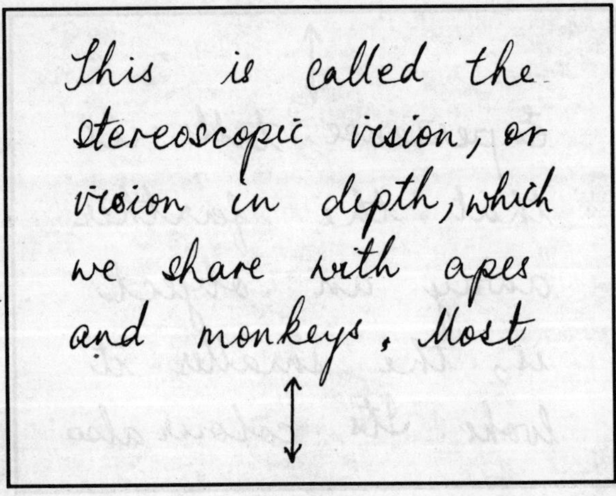

Wide Left Margin

1. Self-respect and high standards.
2. Avoids the past and has courage in facing life.
3. Shy and keeps distance from others.
4. A late riser.

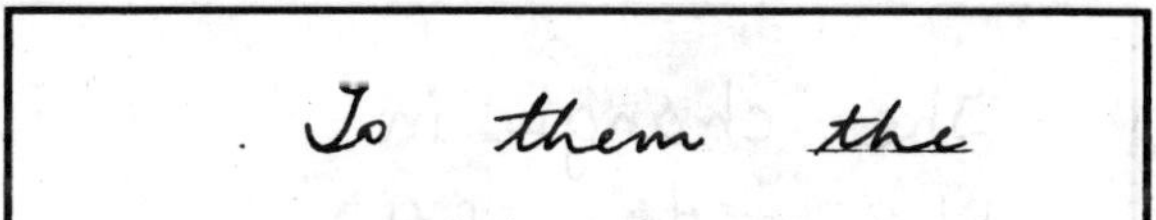

Wide Right Margin

1. Reserved and fearful of future.
2. Oversensitive, self-conscious and fastidious.
3. Extravagant and wasteful.
4. Unrealistic and a poor mixer.

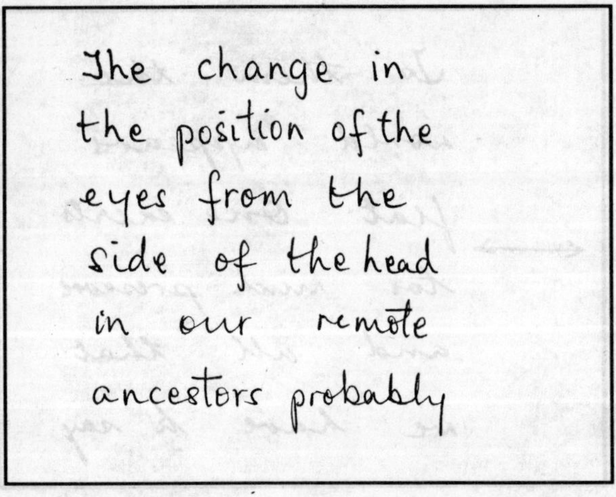

Narrow Upper Margin

1. Informal.
2. Direct.
3. Lack of respect.
4. Indifferent.

thirst is caused by
the body's need for
water. The mouth
feels dry, and
drinking is a but
a natural process
and response, no

Narrow Lower Margin

1. Sentimental and sensuous.
2. Materialistic.
3. Depressed.
4. Communicative.
5. Fatigued.

we smile to show
our pleasures or
amusements in
something or with
someone. In fact,
smiling seems to

Narrow Left Margin

1. Shy and unsociable.
2. Depressed.
3. Lack of spontaneity.
4. Ill-health

> From all directions
> ripples of sound come
> to our ears. Sound
> travels through the
> air, at a speed

Narrow Right Margin

1. Love of travel.
2. Unwise thriftiness.
3. Ambivalent social attitude.

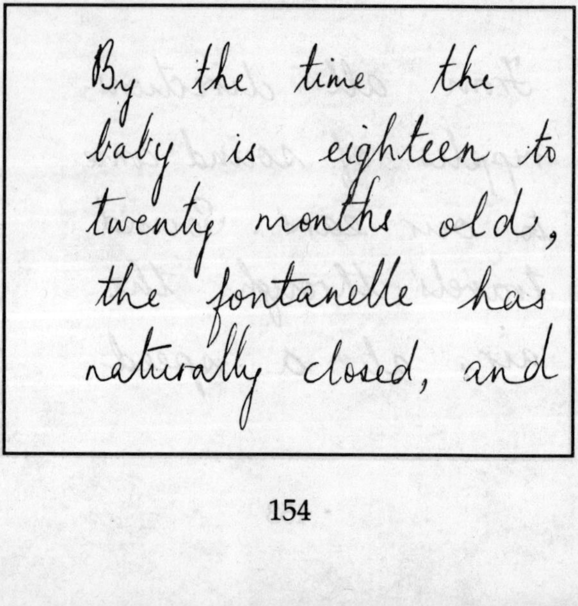

Uneven Margin at Left

1. Rebellious and defiant.
2. Unbalanced and disorganised.
3. Versatile
4. Tolerant.

At the top end
it is attached to
your scapula, or
shoulder blade.
At the elbow, it

Uneven Margin at Right

1. Impulsive.
2. Unreliable reactions.
3. Unwisely thrifty.

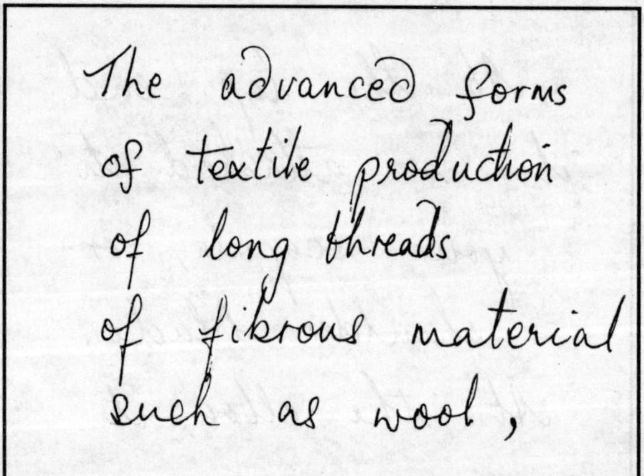

Absence of Margins

1. Insecure and fearful of death.
2. Frugal and stingy.
3. Tactless, talkative and gullible.
4. Kind and hospitable.
5. Fond of luxury and acquisition.
6. Morbidly curious.

> Nowadays, many larger
> farms tend to attack
> such wild animals, and
> they specialise in one
> of the very important
> trades of farming —
> raising crops that pay

Connects and Disconnects

1. Connected writing shows the attitude of the writer towards others.
2. Disconnected writing is a gesture of isolation, of enclosure, and it may lead to attractive new wholes or to withdrawal.

Connected

Good : Analytical, logical and objective, calculating, organised, rational, practical and realistic.

connected

The state of Israel

was established in

nineteen forty-eight.

disconnected

The state of Israel

was established in

nineteen forty-eight.

Bad : Restless, inconsiderate, tactless and compulsive.

Disconnected

Good : Perceptive, intuitive, imaginative, observant, inventive and sensitive.

Bad : Aloof, lonely, insecure, moody, selfish, suspicious, shy, restless, inconsistent, illogical and impractical.